Katie IN SCOTLAND

JAMES MAYHEW

ORCHARD

*For Linda McClelland
and all my friends at the National Galleries
of Scotland
J. M.*

Thanks to:
Piper for her wonderful portrait of Nessie, and to everyone who entered
the Katie Loch Ness Monster art competition; to Orchard Books (as always!);
and to Kate and Faye (whom I met on the train to Edinburgh!) for their tips on
all things Scottish. And thanks to my designer, Tim Rose.

ORCHARD BOOKS
338 Euston Road, London NW1 3BH
Orchard Books Australia
Level 17/207 Kent Street, Sydney, NSW 2000

ISBN 978 1 40833 241 2

First published in 2011 by Orchard Books

This edition published in 2014
Text and illustrations © James Mayhew 2011/2014

The rights of James Mayhew to be identified as the author and
illustrator of this work have been asserted by him in accordance
with the Copyright, Designs and Patents Act, 1988.
A CIP catalogue record for this book is available from the British Library.

2 4 6 8 10 9 7 5 3
Printed in China

Orchard Books is a division of Hachette Children's Books,
an Hachette UK company.
www.hachette.co.uk

Piper Cluness's winning entry for the Loch Ness Monster art competition
can be found on page 28.

KATIE WAS ON HOLIDAY in Scotland with her grandma and her brother Jack. Today they were visiting Loch Ness.

"Do you believe in the Loch Ness Monster?" asked Katie.

"There's no such thing as monsters!" laughed Jack.

He didn't notice the bubbles in the water . . .

A large green creature appeared and said, "No such thing
as monsters? Of course there are!"
"Are you the Loch Ness Monster?" asked Jack.
"Yes! Call me Nessie," she laughed. "Now, what brings you to Scotland?"
"We're on holiday," said Katie.

"You lucky things," sighed Nessie. "I'd love to go on holiday."

"You could come with us," suggested Katie. "Where would you like to go?"

"The Edinburgh Festival," cried Nessie, "to see a show!"

Fortunately, Grandma was the sort of grandma who liked an adventure, so they set off at once. Nessie gave everyone a ride through lochs and rivers to the nearest station.

When they reached the station,
the train driver was very excited.
"What an honour to meet you!"
he said to Nessie.
But Nessie was too big to
get on the train.
"Oh dear," she said. "How
will we get to Edinburgh?"

"Don't worry," said the station
manager. "We've got an old goods
train which should be perfect."
"We'll call it the *Nessie Express*!"
said the train driver. "All aboard!"

Soon they were on their way, rattling past mountains and forests.
It was a beautiful journey.

At last, the train came to a big city called Glasgow. The train driver told them about a wonderful museum called Kelvingrove. It sounded perfect for a small trip so they decided to go and look around.
Nessie was very pleased to find the bones of a long-lost relative inside.

Afterwards, they relaxed in Kelvingrove Park, where Nessie paddled in the river until it was time to get back on the train.

The train took them all the way to Edinburgh.
By the time they arrived it was getting dark.
"Let's find somewhere to spend the night,"
said Grandma.

They found a grand hotel, but Nessie said she preferred
to stay outside.

"I always sleep under the stars," she said.

From their hotel window, Katie and Jack saw her
curled up in a leafy park.

"Goodnight, Nessie," they whispered. "See you tomorrow . . . "

The next day they walked down a street called the Royal Mile.
"Look, it's Nessie!" people shouted. "Are you performing
at the Festival?"
"Go on, Nessie," said Katie. "Why don't you put on
a show tonight?"
"Oh . . . all right, just this once!" said Nessie.
"Hurray!" cheered the crowd.

They set off to explore the city until it was time for the show.

First they came to a grand Royal residence called Holyrood Palace.

"How lovely," said Nessie. "Imagine living here."

"But there's nowhere for you to swim," said Katie.

"That's true," said Nessie. "A loch is better than a palace!"

Next, they found a statue of a small dog called Greyfriars Bobby.

"It says he was a very faithful pet," said Jack, reading the sign.

"I bet you'd be a faithful pet," Katie said to Nessie.

"I would, indeed," smiled Nessie. "But where would you keep me?"

"In the bath!" said Katie, laughing. "Come on, let's go to the castle."

At last, they reached the top of the hill where the castle stood. The other visitors were very excited to see Nessie.

"There's going to be a Nessie show tonight," said Katie. "Don't forget to come along!"

Suddenly, there was a loud BOOM!
"Goodness me! What was that?" cried Nessie.
"The One o'Clock Gun," said a guardsman.
"We fire it every day except Sundays, so
sailors at sea know what the time is."

"Well, I think it's time for lunch," said Grandma, unpacking a picnic. She had even brought some Scottish shortbread as a special treat.
"My favourite!" gasped Nessie.
They sat beside a piper and listened to his bagpipes while they ate.

On their way down from the castle, Nessie
saw a big art gallery.
"I wonder if they have any pictures of me?"
she asked, sticking her nose through the door.
But Katie couldn't see any.
"You'll be needing the Portrait Gallery,"
said a warder.

But there were no pictures of Nessie
in the Portrait Gallery either.

"Never mind, Nessie," said Katie.

"It's nearly time for the show."

"Oh, yes," said Nessie. "How exciting!"

Outside, the crowds were already gathering.

Nessie taught Katie and Jack some Scottish dances.

Soon they were ready for their performance.

"I'm a bit nervous," said Nessie.

"Don't worry, it'll be wonderful," said Katie.

And it was wonderful.
Wearing splendid tartan kilts, they performed in
an open-air theatre. Nessie opened the show with
some Highland Games. She even tossed a caber
while everyone clapped and cheered.

For a grand finale, Nessie sang old Scottish songs while
Katie, Jack and Grandma danced the Highland Fling.
Everyone said it was the best show at the
whole of the Edinburgh Festival.

Afterwards, Katie said, "I've got a surprise for you, Nessie!"
It was a portrait she had drawn all by herself.
"I'm going to give it to the Portrait Gallery," she said.
"Then they'll have a picture of you for everyone to see!"
"It's perfect," said Nessie. "Thank you, Katie."

Grandma said it was getting late – they needed to
catch their train.

"It's time for us to get you back to your loch," she said.
They set off on the *Nessie Express*. They went over
a huge bridge and trundled off through the night,
to the end of the line, where they said goodbye
to the train driver.

By the time they reached Loch Ness it was very late. The scent of heather filled the air and the moon hung low in the sky.

"Do you believe in monsters now?" asked Nessie.

"Definitely," laughed Jack.

"And we always will," said Katie. "Goodbye, Nessie."
And they all waved as Nessie slipped into the dark
waters of the loch and swam out of sight.

Get creative with Katie!

I loved my holiday in Scotland so much that I kept a Scottish sketchbook with all my best pictures inside. I didn't just draw my friend Nessie, I also drew anything else I thought was special, so that I would remember my magical Scottish trip forever.

On your next holiday, why don't you make your own sketchbook and draw all your favourite things from your trip? It will be an amazing way to keep your memories of your holiday together, and I bet your pictures will be terrific!

Love Katie x